There's a
Sparrow
in My Heart

Anthony S. Phillander

Baltimore, Maryland

There's a Sparrow in My Heart

Copyright © 1998 Anthony S. Phillander

All rights reserved under International and Pan-American copyright conventions. No part of this book may be reproduced, stored in a retrieval system, or transmitted in any form, electronic, mechanical, or other means, now known or hereafter invented, without written permission of the publisher. Address all inquiries to the publisher.

This is a work of fiction. All names and characters are either invented or used fictitiously. Any resemblance to persons living or dead is unintentional.

Library of Congress
Cataloging in Publication Data
ISBN 1-56167-434-6

Library of Congress Card Catalog Number:
98-85819

Published by

8019 Belair Road, Suite 10
Baltimore, Maryland 21236

Manufactured in the United States of America

Table of Contents

There's a Sparrow in My Heart 1
I Dreamt a Butterfly Was Kissing Me 2
Gone Again 3
In the Twinkle of an Eye 5
Am Here For You 6
If I Should Ever Lose You 7
Treat Yourself Well 8
My Heart Sings 9
Hero a New Fragrance for Men 10
The Essence of Me 11
Temptation and Desire 12
Your Eyes Are Insinuating 13
For Those Who Love 14
Dying of Love 15
Tremendously 16
Breathtaking in Pink 17
Like My Love a Diamond Is 18
Their Eyes Are on You 19
My Eyes Fell Out My Head 20
For You Time Is Standing Still 21
Everything Everything 22
Hopelessly in Love 23
An Endless Quest for Love 24
Close to My Heart 26
I Will Eat My Heart Out 27
The Answer to Your Need 28
A Celebration of Splendor 29
The Nicest Thing You Have Done for Me 30
A Show of Hearts 31
Am Impassioned About You 32
At the Family Fair 33
Say You Will Be Coming Back Again 34
My Passionate Hunger 35
Be My Guest 36
Princess 37

Kiss Off	38
Intimacy	39
What You Might Have Been	40
Listen to Them	41
For a Moment	42
Have Got It It's In Me	43
No Need for Rain	44
On the Catwalk	45
It's Imperative	46
The Lady in My Life	47
Difficult But Not Impossible	48
Don't Keep Pushing Me Away	49
Yours Forever	50
Am Lost in You and Me	51
Man's Inhumanity to Man	52
One Sweet Squeeze	54
One Look Says It All	56
"Knowledge Is Power"	57
You Are Too Sweet	58
In an Intimate Embrace	59
She's Got Fashion Sense	60
Come Home	61
Feel the Heat	62
Don't Despair	63
Magical Mysterious Magnificent	64
Living a Colorful Life	65
A Good Thing	66
Romantically Inclined	67
Go Back to School	68
You Are an Original	69
A Cell of Your Love	70
My Perpetual Obsession	71
Hear Your Voice	72
Waiting for You in My Mind	73
Your Heart Is My Accomplice	74
Part Invitation Part Intimidation	75
Don't Keep Your Passion Bottled Up Inside	76
Have Got a Guilty Conscience	77

This Thing of Ours	78
Slippery When Wet	79
Take Action	80
Enthusiasm	81
Smile It's Catching	82
Clear the Air	84
We Are Number One	85
The Road to Success	86
Reach for Your Future	87
Sexy Seductive Sensual	88
This Is Your Moment	89
Fresh Look	90
Achievers	91
A Dream Denied	92
If You Want It	93
With You in Mind	94
Where Friends Meet	95
High and Dry	96
It's Now Overdue	97
Coming Soon	98
All of a Sudden	99
A Passion for Learning	100
More to You Than Meets the Eye	101

There's a Sparrow in My Heart

There's a sparrow in my heart
which is constantly singing very sweetly
and the closer you get to me
its melody increases in intensity

since you came to me
it's been constantly keeping me company
like you I will never set it free
'cause I am immensely enjoying its sweet melody

There's a sparrow in my heart
which is constantly singing very sweetly
the closer you are to me
sweeter is the sound of its reverie

You came to me and from that moment
it has been singing merrily
you put a sparrow in my heart
and it is sweetly singing to me constantly

There's a sparrow in my heart
and they are singing in harmony
singing just like you and me
there's a sparrow in my heart

You put a sparrow in my heart
there's a sparrow in my heart
a sparrow's in my heart
there's a sparrow in my heart.

I Dreamt a Butterfly Was Kissing Me

I dreamt a butterfly was kissing me
and someone once told me if I should ever dream
that I am being kissed by a butterfly
I will meet a new lady and now you have come to me

Before you came to me
I did not believe in fairy tales or dreams
then I had this dream and you appeared
now you have made a believer out of me

I dreamt a butterfly was kissing me
then I remembered what someone told me
if you ever dream you are being kissed by a butterfly
no doubt about it soon you will meet a new ladylove

You made a dream believer out of me
the moment you appeared the dream became reality
you are here kissing and loving me
and I am forever living in a dream

I dreamt a butterfly was kissing me
now I no longer need to dream
'cause you are here with me.

Gone Again

Gone again she's gone again
just when I was beginning to think that this time
this time she was back to stay forever
I came home and I discovered
she and all her things is missing yes she's gone again

She came back and I was happy as a lark
this time I thought we had finally gotten
our act together
we talked heart-to-heart about our love
and what went wrong the first time
now she's gone and I am sad

Gone again she's gone again
just when I was beginning to think
that this time she was here to stay forever
I don't have a clue
don't know the reason but she's gone again

She came back and I was in seventh heaven
I thought that forever we could have held it together
this time
after we discussed and decided to compromise
'cause we are like fishes out of water
without each other
now she's gone

Gone again she's gone again
I came home and could not believe what I was seeing
she and all of her things are missing
I don't want to believe it
still it's true gone again she's gone again

She's gone again
She's gone again
gone again
again.

In the Twinkle of an Eye

In the twinkle of an eye love changed my life
now my heart is all smiles
'cause she smiled and her smile
stayed in my heart

I was not looking for love
still love found me in the twinkle of an eye
when she so innocently smiled at me
brought joy into my heart and into my life

In the twinkle of an eye
love changed my life
now my heart is all smiles am happy and satisfied
she smiled and her smile stayed in my heart

I was no longer looking for love
'cause I had grown tired and stopped
after having tried for most of my life
despair was now in my eyes

In the twinkle of an eye
love found me and changed my life
in the twinkle of an eye
love came bringing joy into my life

In the twinkle of an eye
in the twinkle of an eye
twinkle of an eye.

Am Here For You

Am here for you
forever this is where
time will find me here
taking good and loving care of you

Never you worry your sweet head
although I know time has a way of running away
I will not follow
by your side I will always stay

Am here for you and forever
I will never venture out of your view
am always within your reach and touch
'cause I love you oh so very much

Never you worry your sweet head
darling put your fears and tears to bed
for you I am and I will always be right here
dear your lover ain't going anywhere

Am here for you
staying here for you
am here for you
for you am here

Am here for you

If I Should Ever Lose You

I will leave no stone unturned
I will disturb each and every grain of sand
I will circumnavigate the globe
I will reach beyond the universe

If I should ever lose you
these things I will do and even more
for you are worth more than anything
this world can ever give to me

I will search the innermost submerged depths
of the sea
I will look behind the moon to bring you back to me
I will cool the sun and take a look around
I will ask the father in heaven to return you to me

If I should ever lose you all these things I will do
nothing will be impossible for me
'cause without you I cannot be
don't let me have to go through this trouble
forever stay with me

I will work miracles to bring you back to me
if I should ever lose you
I will do the impossible to bring you back to me
I will bring you back to me.

Treat Yourself Well

Treat yourself well dispel the notion
that you do not deserve the best 'cause you do
in your life you are the most important person
so treat yourself with reverence be good to yourself

Stop playing second fiddle
to everyone else's needs and desires
don't you have needs and desires too
do not wait for anyone to treat you
like you ought to be
do it for yourself no one will treat you like you will

Treat yourself well the standard by which
you have got to love your neighbour is as yourself
if you love yourself then you will treat yourself well
then that love and good treatment
you can extend to your neighbour

Stop putting everything and everyone before you
you are just as good as everyone else so be good to you
you are worth it and you know deep down
that you deserve it
you should be first in your life you better believe it

Treat yourself well
banish the notion that you are selfish
you are very important so stop settling for seconds
you are the number one person in your life no fooling
treat yourself well you deserve it you are worth it

Treat yourself well
treat yourself well
treat yourself well

My Heart Sings

My lover my heart sings
every time it hears your name
when you came to me
my very world you changed

How well I remember
that day when you came
my heart was and will forever be inflamed even after
kingdom has come and gone away

My lover your every wish is my command
you do not need to lead me into temptation
just keep leading me to your heaven
and forever I will call your name
and my heart will sing your praise

I remember very well
that day when you came 'cause
my heart was and will
forever remain inflamed with this passion for your love

My lover my heart sings
my heart sings every time I hear your name
every time I hear your name my heart sings
my heart sings every time I hear your name

My heart sings.

Hero a New Fragrance for Men

Hero a new fragrance for men
that is what she gave to me
then she told me I was her champion
her hero and she knew
forever I will take care of her

Am her champion her hero
now have got to live up to her ideal even if
with my wandering ways I wish to continue
have got to be her hero her champion
and never leave her

Hero a new fragrance for men she presented
telling me I am her champion her hero
a goodwill gesture a token of her affection
she is giving to remind me that I am her man

Hero a new fragrance for men
got me feeling like a hero and a champion
I adore her forever I will be staying with
protecting and taking loving care of her

Hero a new fragrance for men
got my heart in chains
hero a new fragrance for men
a new fragrance for men

The Essence of Me

You are the essence of me
the essence of style charm and beauty
forever I will be grateful to destiny
for bringing you to me

I was merely existing until you came to me
before you there weren't really me
a figment I was a figment until you came to me
I was merely an illusion

You are the very essence of me
the essence of style
sophistication charm and beauty
I thank the day when destiny brought you my way

Before you there was no me
a figment a mere illusion
that's all I was really
then you came to me

The essence of me
you are the essence of me
you are the very essence of me
the essence of me.

Temptation and Desire

You are temptation
you are desire
my heart's yielding to your temptation
I am surrendering to my desire

Everything about you is desirable
you are also intriguing and truly remarkable
you are just outstanding the way you are looking
even the angels in heaven will yield to you
and am just a man

You are temptation
you are desire
my heart has no other option
but to yield to your temptation
then without hesitation am surrendering to my desire

Everything about you is desirable
you are remarkable intriguing and so interesting
am in awe I want to quickly get closer to you
this fire in my heart burns intensely all because of you

Temptation and desire
you are nothing but temptation and desire
my heart has already yielded to your temptation
have got to fulfill my desire for you

Temptation and desire
you are nothing but
temptation and desire
temptation and desire.

Your Eyes Are Insinuating

If your eyes are insinuating
what I think they are insinuating
then wait a minute hold it right there
come over here and prove it

It is possible that they could be right
then again it's possible that they are wrong
we will never know until we put it to the test
put it to the test come over here
and look me in the eye

If your eyes are insinuating
just what I think they are insinuating
don't wait another minute no don't even blink
this instant come over here and prove it

It is possible that they could be right
by the same token they could be wrong
you will never know my true feelings if you don't
come over here and try proving
what your eyes are hinting

Your eyes are insinuating that I am
am stopping and that
the rest am leaving up to you
prove just what your eyes are insinuating

Your eyes are insinuating?

For Those Who Love

For those who love they say
time is eternity then it goes without saying
because of the love between you and me
we will be loving for eternity

Time is relative according to your activity
and we are enjoying loving you and me
so time is of no consequence
time is really of no concern to you and me

For those who love
time they say is eternity
so you and me we will never have to worry
our love is guaranteed to last for eternity

Time is relative according to your activity
we are in love and being in love brings us such joy
that time does not matter
to you and me

We are in love and for eternity
deep in love we are destined to be
for those who love they say time is eternity
and with what they say we wholeheartedly agree

For those who love they say time is eternity.

Dying of Love

Love am dying of love
and the only cure for what is ailing me
is the very said thing which is
slowly taking the breath of life from me

The remedy for my affliction
is the same thing which is causing my condition
am in a quandary love is killing me
and I need it urgently to save me

Love am dying of love
and the only cure for what is ailing me
is the very said thing which is
slowly taking the breath of life from me

The remedy for my affliction
is the same thing which is responsible for my condition
am in a terrible situation
urgently I need love got to have love in a big hurry

Love am dying from lack of love
have got to have love in great quantities
only love can restore my life to me
give me love let the breath of life stay with me

Love am dying from love deprivation
love am dying of love
dying of love.

Tremendously

Tremendously that's the only way I can love you
for have got a tremendous heart
so again you won't have to ask
'cause now am sure you know how much I do

Not only sincerely
not only for a billion reasons
not only because of your spellbinding beauty
but tremendously I love you tremendously

Tremendously it's the only way I can love you
that's the only way I can love you
because of my tremendous heart
you won't have to ask again
'cause now I have made it as plain as day

Not only for the twinkle in your eyes
or that magnificent glow in your smile
nor the passion in your touch
when you ever so passionately touch me
ask me again how much I love you

Tremendously end of story
I love you tremendously
I love you tremendously
tremendously.

Breathtaking in Pink

Breathtaking in pink
you look breathtaking in pink and to think
everyone's saying you look beautiful
how blind can they be
can't they see you are just breathtaking

Outstanding elegant sophisticated shall I go on
exciting tantalizing thrilling mesmerizing
wow pink really got you in the pink
pink sure does a lot of things for you

Breathtaking in pink
you are simply breathtaking in pink
I am sure whatever color you choose to wear
will suit you
but in pink you look magnificent

Outstanding elegant sophisticated astonishing
If anyone say you are looking pretty pay them no mind
that's an understatement darling in pink
you look wonderful
yes dear you are truly breathtaking in pink

Not just pretty you are breathtaking in pink
breathtaking in pink
breathtaking.

Like My Love a Diamond Is

My love is forever
like a diamond is and always will be
so forget about diamonds
take my love let it be your best friend

The jewel of your lifetime
everything that any girl could ever want it is
it will make you shine from inside out
then diamonds you won't really have any need of

My love is forever
like a diamond is and always will be forever
with my love you don't need diamonds
still I will buy you the largest I can find
so you can compare it with my love

The jewel of your life
anything that you want me to be take my love
and I will become forever like a diamond
that's how my love is
go on take it and it will be your best friend

My love is like a diamond is
yes it's forever.

Their Eyes Are on You

All the guys got their eyes on you
your animal magnetism is attracting them
like butterflies to beautiful flowers in a flower garden
and don't talk about that perpetual come-on look
in your eyes

They will willingly do whatever you want them to
and things which you never ask them to do
they will do also just because they all want to
get much closer to you

All the guys got their eyes on you
your animal magnetism and that perpetual come-on look
in your eyes
is simply driving all of them wild
like butterflies to a flower they are being drawn to you

They will willingly do anything you ask them to
you are their queen your unspoken wish
is their command
stop letting them suffer in silence
tell them you are already taken tell them you are mine

Their eyes are on you
all the guys got their eyes on you
their eyes are on you
they got their eyes on you.

My Eyes Fell Out My Head

My eyes fell out my head
I had to pick my tongue from off the floor
my knees refused to hold me anymore
the first time you came into the store

You are so beautiful
I even mistook you for that movie star
her first name is Mellisa her last name
right now I cannot rightly remember

My eyes fell out my head
I had to pick my tongue from off the floor
the first time you walked through that door
I knew I just could not let you walk away
without saying hello

You are a head turner
you have got my heart pulsing
faster than a high frequency radio transmitter
my eyes are a gyroscope and they are focused on you

My eyes fell out my head
my feet simply refused to carry me any further
the moment I saw you I knew forever
forever if it took forever I had to be with you

Now here you are.

For You Time Is Standing Still

Although time lines are
unnoticeably constantly being placed upon your face
you still retain this youthfulness
this timeless graciousness
you are still a masterpiece of feminine magnificence

You have got time where you want it to be
in the palm of your hand
and it compliments you magnificently
it's doing exactly what you told it to
for you time is standing still

Although the lines of time are
beginning to leave traces upon your face
you are still in command of your timeless gracefulness
you are still elegant you are forever
a masterpiece of feminine charm

You have got time in the palm of your hands
you are making it follow your explicit instructions
to you it is extremely obedient baby congratulations
you have got time marking time for you
time is standing still

Time is gentle with you
you still got this youthfulness
this timeless graciousness
you are still a masterpiece of feminine magnificence
a masterpiece of feminine magnificence

For you time is standing still
still standing still
time is for you.

Everything Everything

Everything everything
I will give you everything you want
within reason of course
then again why should I limit you let me give you
everything within and beyond reason

Nothing is too much for me to give to you
everything you want let me give to you
the sky is not the limit when it comes to you
if you desire heaven just make a wish
and I will bring it to you

Everything everything
everything you want I will give to you be unreasonable
go on ask me for the moon let me bring it to you
let me prove what I am saying
is the honest to goodness truth

Nothing is too much for me to give to you
including all my sincere love
and a lifetime of devotion too
ask for whatever you desire don't be afraid to ask
ask me and I will cheerfully give everything to you

Everything everything
ask for everything you desire
and I will be only too happy
to give it to you ask for everything you want
let me give everything you want to you
ask for everything

Everything.

Hopelessly in Love

Say yes am hoping beyond hope
hoping that you feel the same way about me
the way am feeling about you
'cause you see am hopeless
am hopelessly in love with you

How this happened I haven't got a clue
all of a sudden out of the blue
I started feeling things for you things
things which I haven't felt for anyone else before

Say yes I don't think I will be able
to take no for an answer
am hoping beyond hope that you feel
the same way about me
the way am feeling about you am hoping beyond hope
hoping that you are hopelessly in love with me too

Hopelessly in love and hoping beyond hope
am hoping beyond hope am hopelessly in love
am hopelessly in love and hoping beyond hope
hoping that you are hopelessly in love with me also

Hopeless yes am hopelessly in love with you
and am hoping
hoping that you are hopelessly in love with me too
hopeless in love hopelessly in love
hopelessly in love with you.

An Endless Quest for Love

Am on an endless quest for love
every time I enter love's circle and like
a merry-go-round it starts spinning around
once again love always manages to bypass me

And once again from up on high
am down in the drain and wondering why
over and over again have got to start
start looking for love all over and over again

Am on an endless quest for love
again and again it keeps happening
every time I enter love's circle
like a merry-go-round it begins to spin around
and again love manages to bypass me

And again from up on high
am down in the drain in pain and beginning to start
start wondering why I always have to start
start looking for love all over again

Am on an endless quest for love
what am I doing wrong why can't I find
the right someone to settle me down
I can't understand why
and my love life keeps going round and around

Am on an endless quest for love
the journey has become very tiresome
in a hurry I need to find the right someone to love
would you by any chance need someone

would you do you need someone
end my quest for love.

Close to My Heart

I will wear your love in and close to my heart
no one else will be able to get any closer
every part of it will eternally be reserved for you
yes forever that's how it will be

You don't have to worry you will never be sorry
it will always be secure and very safe with me
come on stop holding back bring it to here
yes give your love to me

I will wear it wear your love in and close to my heart
no one else will ever be able to get any closer
every part of my heart will be
eternally reserved for you forever
I promise you forever that's how it will forever be

You don't know you don't have to worry
it will always be safe and very secure with me
stop being like that stop holding back
give it come give your love to me

Close to my heart
I will wear your love
close to my heart
come on now present it to me.

I Will Eat My Heart Out

I will eat my heart out
grief will make me eat my heart out
if our love should ever fizzle and die out
the grief will eat my heart out

Stop I don't want to talk about it anymore
for if it ever happens it will surely be the end of me
no I don't even want to think about it
your love is everything to me

I will eat my heart out
grief will make me eat my heart out
if our love should ever come undone
I pray it never happens
for the grief yes the grief will make me
eat my heart out

Stop it no don't talk about it anymore
change the subject
just thinking about it is bringing me down
just the thought of it is hurting me so
your love have got to have your love forevermore

Eat my heart out I will eat my heart out
if I ever have to live without you
I will eat my heart out
grief will make me eat my heart out if I ever lost you.

The Answer to Your Need

Stop no longer do you have to
search beg and keep pleading for love
'cause am here to fill your every need
raise your head look at me am the answer to your need

I will fill your need
you can put your mind at ease
no you don't have to worry
worry about ever again being lonely

Stop no longer do you have to
keep searching begging pleading
for love on bended knees
you have just filled your need am here for you
am the answer to your need

Am the answer to your need
question me and I will begin to fill you in
am the answer to your need
the answer to your need is me

Am the answer to your need.

A Celebration of Splendor

You are a celebration of splendor
so out going so full of glamor
my heart bows before you
I can't help but fall helplessly in love with you

You have got a sparkling demeanor
with you when I am with you
excitement is always on the agenda
not even for a moment from you
do I want to wander far

A celebration of splendor
you are a celebration of splendor
graceful elegant and oh so very charming
nothing will give me more pleasure
than spending my lifetime with you

A celebration of splendor
you are a magnificent and beautiful
celebration of splendor
a celebration a celebration of splendor.

The Nicest Thing You Have Done for Me

The nicest thing you have ever done for me
the nicest thing you have ever done for me
is everything which you keep doing daily
including sincerely loving me

Keep doing those nice things
you are daily doing for me
everything you do for me is a nicest thing
I really can't single out a specific one immediately

The nicest thing you have ever done for me
the nicest thing you have ever done for me
is each and every little single thing
which you keep daily doing for me
'cause you do them willing and lovingly

Keep doing those nice things you are daily doing for me
everything you do for me is a nicest thing really
you are so nice to me I really can't single out one really
everything you do for me is the nicest thing

The nicest thing you have ever done for me
you really want to know well let's see
the nicest thing you have done for me is
giving all your love to me

Really it is the nicest thing you have ever done for me
giving your love to me is the nicest thing
it is the nicest thing you have ever done for me
giving your love to me.

A Show of Hearts

Let's have a show of hearts
I will show you mine and you can show me yours
am in favor of loving you and you are
in favor of loving me
let's have a show of hearts before we agree to fall in
love

We will pass a motion to always show emotion
in this love we will not withhold affection
since there's no further discussion
concerning our emotional situation
it's now a forgone conclusion our love can now begin

Let's have a show of hearts
so that the motion of our loving each other for a lifetime
can be witnessed and agreed upon by the both of us
am in favor of loving you
and you are in favor of loving me

Are we both in favor of loving each other for a lifetime
you bet then it's a forgone conclusion
this love of our's will have no termination
one more time let's have a show of hearts

Let's have a show of hearts.

Am Impassioned About You

Am impassioned about you my main purpose
my passion in life is you life has no meaning
no reason to go on living without you
it's true am impassioned about you

Everything else is second to you
what is my life if I can't live it with you
how can I live if am not living with you
why should I go on living without you
give me one good reason

Am impassioned about you my passion in life is you
you are my only purpose too without you life
life has no meaning no reason to keep living
am telling you 'cause I want to make certain
that you know

Everyone else in my life comes after you
what is my life if I can't live it with you
how can I live when without you I will forever be blue
girl that will not be possible

Am impassioned about you
am impassioned about you
am impassioned about
impassioned about you.

At the Family Fair

At the family fair
it was at the family fair in the market square
there my eyes first met her and she
effortlessly took my breath away

Like a beautiful rose in a floral bouquet
she stood out amongst all those flowers
which were on display
then my heart began playing a melody
which am still hearing up to this day

At the family fair
it was at the family fair that sunny day
in the market square
there's where my eyes first met her
and from that day I haven't looked away

Like a beautiful rose in a floral bouquet she stood out
she still stands out to this day
as she was standing out
that day amongst the flowers which were on display
in the market square when she took my breath away

My heart's still playing the same melody it played
when my eyes first met her
and she took my breath away
I met a dream at the family fair
at the family fair I met a dream.

Say You Will Be Coming Back Again

Am badmouthing your name since you been gone
am feeling no pain with my lips
those words I keep repeating
but if my heart could have spoken right now
it would have been telling a totally different story

My heart's so sorry it misses you dearly
so to ease the strain my lips sways to ease my pain
still with all those words am saying
if you was to only say
say you are coming back again with open arms
I will welcome you

Am badmouthing your name
but I know it's a straight case of sour grapes
I know now that I am the only one to blame
am responsible for your leaving
and am so ashamed am sorry

My heart's in pain I don't know why
I let things get so far out of hand when you were here
the world was mine to command now you are gone and
I am twisting in the wind when will it end

I don't know how to begin saying this
but I need a second chance
come back let's try again
say you will be coming back again

My heart's in pain.

My Passionate Hunger

You are my passionate hunger
the more I keep hungering for you
the pangs keeps getting stronger and I don't think
I can go on suffering much longer

Have tried many other
in my quest to satiate my hunger
still all those others which have tried were unable to
make and keep me satisfied so on you
have still got my eyes

You are my passionate hunger
I thought in time I would have gotten over you
but as time passes by I find this hunger
which am hungering for you is growing stronger

Have tried but it makes no sense
for me to keep on trying to satisfy
my hunger with any others
for I know now that I won't ever be satisfied
until I satisfy my hunger for you with you

You are my passionate hunger
only you can satisfy this passion in me
I will never be satisfied until I have you
I will never be satisfied.

Be My Guest

Be my guest in my heart
in my heart you can stay for as long as you desire
still am extending this special invitation
I will be truly honored if you choose to stay forever

Yes my heart is big so always having you around
will never pose any problems to me
am hoping you will say yes and accept my invitation
this invitation which am so generously extending to you

Be my guest my heart is at your disposal
you can stay for as long as you desire
still I will much rather that you stay forever
it will be my greatest pleasure
having you in my heart forever

My heart's big enough to accommodate you
it no problem having you
I will be honored if forever in my heart
you decided to stay

Stay in my heart forever
be my guest
yes be my guest forever
be my guest forever

Be my guest.

Princess

Princess when you left
you did not say good-bye
yet we understand
still you did not leave any one of us with dry eyes

You left us high and dry
we were not looking forward
to so soon being without you
suddenly we turned around and you are in heaven

Princess is it true that they do
if so why do the good so quickly pass on
we were planing to have you around
for a very long time
suddenly you are gone leaving us
disappointed and despondent

You left us high and dry
now there's water in our eyes as we keep
wondering why
why did heaven call you home so soon
did heaven miss you
as much as we are now missing you

Princess it was so nice having you around
now in our hearts forever you will live on
enjoy your forever in heaven
Diana we are missing you we are missing you princess

Princess we are missing you.

Kiss Off

Kiss and hold me tight
tonight give me your love and I will
indelibly imprint it on my heart and from now
until the end of time it will never kiss off

Like an eternal flame
in my heart it will shine
and forever keep burning bright
showing me its light

Kiss and hold me tight
give me your love
with your kiss indelibly imprint it on my heart
and not even with the passing of time will it kiss off

Like an eternal flame
deep in my heart burning very bright
there eternally it will stay day and night
for and beyond my earthly life

Kiss me and seal the love
which you have indelibly imprinted on my heart
seal it strong and when you do
forever it will remain and never kiss off

Kiss me with your kiss seal your love in my heart
forever it will be a part of me.

Intimacy

Tonight am all alone here
dreaming of you and me and the intimacy we shared
when you were here
when you still cared

Tomorrow it will be the same way
me all alone everywhere I go I will still be
daydreaming of you and me and the intimacy
we used to share when you was still here

Tonight am all alone here
still dreaming of you and me again like I was
dreaming of you and me the night before
and the intimacy
we shared cause back then you still cared

Tomorrow again I know it's going to be the same way
me all alone everywhere I go I will still be
daydreaming of you and me and the intimacy
we are not sharing anymore
and again my heart will start shedding tears

It's the story of my life
every night since you have been gone
am lying all alone here
missing you and the intimacy we shared
'cause now no one cares

Am missing you and the intimacy
we are not sharing anymore
tonight my heart's in shreds
my heart's in shreds.

What You Might Have Been

They say it's never too late
never too late to be what you might have been
you are still living aren't you
everyone of you aren't you
so what's the problem

What do you think you might have been
could have been would like to have been
have got news for you all friends you all still can
you can still become whatever you think
you could have been

They say it's never too late
to be what you might have been
so long as you all can hear what this song is saying
am speaking to all of you my friends are you with me
listen you can still become what you might have been

what do you think you might have been
could have been would like to have been
if you already know what you could have been
then right now start doing something to become
what you think you could have been
because you can be

You can still become what you think
you might have been could have been
would you like to be go on make that dream a reality
the fat lady hasn't even begun to sing for you

It's never too late they say it's never too late
never too late to become what you would like to be
yes you still got time but you must take action
so begin it's never too late never too late.

Listen to Them

Listen to them
listen to the hammers of my heart
listen to the hammers of my heart as they beat out
beats out a melody of love for us to sing and dance to

Can you hear it
listen carefully and a celestial symphony
you will hear playing in harmony
as it beats out a heavenly melody

Listen to them
listen to the hammers of my heart
listen to the hammers of my heart as they beats out
beats out a melody of love enticing us
to become romantically involved

Listen carefully can you hear it
listen and you will hear a celestial symphony
playing in harmony listen carefully
can you hear it are you hearing the melody

Let's dance you and me as we
listen to this heavenly symphony playing sweetly
as it plays the melody in our melody of love
dance baby for a lifetime dance with me

Dance with me keep dancing to our melody.

For a Moment

For a moment I lose concentration
then I have to stop so that I ask myself
where I am again 'cause I was like I always am
deep in thoughts of you

I don't know why
but somehow with thoughts of you
I easily gets carried away it's true
that's the effect you are having on me

For a moment am just saying that
but it's not true cause every moment
am thinking of you
then there are moments when I realizes that am lost
and tries to force myself to stop thinking of you
every moment

You your smile your voice your mannerism
thinking about you your beauty and your mannerism
always carries me away carries me back
back to the first day I met you

For a moment
for a moment there I was lost
there's not a moment when am not lost
in thoughts of you
from the day I met you have been lost in thoughts
of you

for a moment.

Have Got It It's In Me

Have got it it's in me
it moves me shakes me rocks and rolls me
twists and twirls me inside outside and round about
I can't stand still cause it controls me

It's in me nothing I can do about it
am always at its mercy
have got to do what it make me
willingly go wherever it takes me

Have got it it's in me
it moves me shakes me rattles me rolls me
twirls twists and turns me out inside
and round all about
I can't sit still cause it controls me

It's in me nothing I can do about it
am always at its every whim and fancy
have got to do what it wants me
obediently do what it tells me

Have got it it's in me
it's music to my ears and I like it it's in me
from my head to toes in my heart and soul
and each and every single bone in my body

Have got it it's in me.

No Need for Rain

No I will have no need for rain
never again in my life will I ever
have any need for rain again no never again
not with this deluge of tears my eyes are crying

Since she's been gone not for one solitary moment
did it ever stop flowing
with no hope of her returning
I don't think there's a possibility of it ever subsiding

No no I will have no need for rain
never again in my life will I ever have
any need for rain
no on no never again will I have any need
for rain again
never again not with this deluge of tears am crying

She's been gone since she's been gone
not for one solitary moment not once
did it ever stop flowing and with no hope
of her ever returning
there's no possibility of it ever subsiding

So I will have no need for rain
I will have no need for rain
'cause since she's been gone
my heart has been and is still crying
my heart's crying since she's been gone
my heart's crying

No need no need for rain.

On the Catwalk

On the catwalk she parades and poses
if she only wink at you
without hesitation you are in a hurry
to do what you think her wink supposes

In her eyes resides an open invitation to her tenderness
if you happen to be the lucky one
to gain possession of her invitation
listen carefully you will hear your heart purring

On the catwalk she parades and poses
in clothes of all descriptions color shapes and sizes
when she ever so innocently sends her smile your way
instantly she will put you in the mood
to send her roses

In her voice is sultry seduction
if she whispers in your ear and extends an invitation
listen your heart is beginning to growl
growl like a lion

On the catwalk she moves like a panther
but in your arms she's a model of a woman
she moves like a tiger on the catwalk
but in your arms she's a tender little kitten

On the catwalk she parades and poses.

It's Imperative

I need your smile
to shed its light on my life
I need your eyes for when I look into them
happiness is all I see residing inside

Don't deny me what I need
without it I can't survive
it's imperative that you provide these things
which I dearly need or I will die

I need your touch to warm me inside and out
I need your arms to hold me day and night
I need your lips to kiss and your voice
to sing to me I don't want much

Don't deny me what I need is all I ask
what I really need is you
you can fill all my needs
it's imperative that I have you

Imperative that I have you imperative
it's imperative.

The Lady in My Life

The lady in my life
don't let her hear me telling you this
'cause it will lift her head
way up high

Without her I will not be living a life
she's the light of my eyes
the beat of my heart
truly she's my breath of life

The lady in my life
I don't know why but when am away from her
time just seems to drag and
a deep sadness completely fills my heart

Without her I won't have life
she's the light of my eyes
the beat of my heart
she's my fresh breath of life

I won't live if she's not in my life
the lady in my life am deep in love
and so very proud of her
from now to beyond eternity
I will be looking in her eyes.

Difficult But Not Impossible

Very often if you are brave enough and dare to try
surprising you will find that
yes your challenges are indeed difficult
but not impossible for you to overcome

Perception it's all in the perception
when you really put your mind to it
even Mt. Everest is not impossible for you to climb
so take heart and give it a try

Often very often if you are brave enough
and dare to try
when you are finally successful
to your amazement you will wonder why
wonder why you did not try all the time

Perception it's all in the perception of the situation
oh the things you can do if you will only begin
yes try and when you are successful
it will blow your mind wow now you know

Your challenges may be difficult
difficult but not impossible to overcome
difficult but not impossible to overcome
difficult but not impossible to surmount

Impossible! impossible is only a state of mind
Difficult but not impossible.

Don't Keep Pushing Me Away

Don't keep pushing me away
'cause no matter what I do try as I may
I just cannot stand to be away from you
I need to be wherever you are

The way you treat me you should be
immediately arrested for mental cruelty
yet still silly me if the law should ever hold you
I will the first one pleading to set you free

Don't you keep pushing me away
I keep running to you
you keep turning and running away from me
If I had any mind
I would have forgotten about you a long time ago
but for me
that's hopelessly impossible to do

Don't you keep pushing me away are you blind
can't you see that I am insanely in love with you
am insanely in love with you
but you keep pushing me away
don't you keep pushing me away don't push me away

Don't you keep pushing me away

Yours Forever

Yours forever my heart's yours forever
surrender your heart to me and together
we will build a love that's stronger
than any love the world has ever known before

Juliet and Romeo Anthony and Cleopatra
Delilah and Sampson
The Duke of Windsor and Mrs. Simpson
even their strong love won't be able to compare
with the love we will build together

Yours forever my heart's yours forever
surrender your heart to me
together we will build a love that's much stronger
than all those legendary loves which have gone before

Solomon and Sheba The Shah Jahan
whose love for Mumtaz
inspired him to build the Taj Mahal
Delilah and Sampson
The Duke Of Windsor and Mrs. Simpson
their's were strong loves but ours will be much stronger

Mine's yours forever now come surrender
surrender your heart to me
surrender your heart to me
mine's already yours forever

surrender yours to me.

Am Lost in You and Me

Follow me am lost too am lost in you follow me
let's get lost in you and me am already lost in you
come on follow and get lost in me too am lost in you
am already lost in you

So far gone into you
am so far gone into you don't know where you end
and I begin
but we are joined and yet we are not always one
so far gone into you am far gone

Follow me am lost too am lost in you
follow me and we will get lost in you and me
am already lost in you follow me and
let's get lost in you and me

So far gone into you
lost way into you am already lost
follow me and let's get lost in you and me
let's get lost in you and me

Follow me am lost.

Man's Inhumanity to Man

Man's inhumanity to man tell me friend
when will it end
have looked at the past now am looking into the future
still I cannot see the answer to the reasons why
man is still being tremendously inhuman
to his fellow man

The world seems to be in a perpetual war
the moment it ceases in one place
the next instant it flares-up in another and so
this viciousness continues to remain unbroken

Man's inhumanity to man
man inhumanity to man everywhere I look I can find
another glaring example of the destruction
man continues to inflict upon his fellow man

The world is I a perpetual state of war
we are suppose to love one another
not destroy each other
mankind what are we fighting for
forever we have been searching
and up to this time no one has found the answer

Man's inhumanity to man
why is man so inhuman to his brother man
why can't we change direction join hands
and try to find
find a solution to this universal problem

Question is are we willing to do something
to put and end
to this way of living or forever continue

to give lip service
until the fall of the final curtain
when awe are all going up in flames

Man's inhumanity to man
has the world on the edge of annihilation
man's inhumanity to man
is causing universal devastation.

One Sweet Squeeze

One sweet squeeze she's got one sweet squeeze
her arms must be made of honey 'cause when she
wraps those arms around me I feel sweet
my knees gets weak and all my lips can say
is honey please

She's a real tease the girl's a real tease
nothing pleases her more
than to have me on my knees
pleading please honey please whatever you do
don't stop
please don't stop loving me

One sweet squeeze she's got one sweet squeeze
her arms got to be made of honey
whenever she holds me
I feel sweet my knees gets weak I can hardly speak
and my lips merely whisper honey please

She's a tease the girl's a real tease
she knows she has got me and I love
her arms around me
she knows that I love her squeeze that's why
she loves to squeeze and bring me to my knees
she loves to hear me

She loves to have me pleading please honey please
don't stop whatever you do don't you ever stop
don't you dare stop loving me
one sweet squeeze she's got one sweet squeeze

One sweet squeeze
it's sweet sweet sweet one sweet squeeze
she's got one sweet squeeze squeeze
sweet squeeze.

One Look Says It All

One look says it all
words aren't necessary at all
one look says it all you said it with one look
then you did not have to say a single word

You made me feel a million miles tall
my heart heard and answered when your eyes called
your eyes called and my heart heard and answered
when you gave me one look

One look says it all
words aren't necessary at all
one look says it all you said it with one look
then you didn't have to say a single word

You made me feel a million miles tall
my heart heard and answered when you call
your eyes called my heart heard and answered
when you gave me one look

One look says it all
you gave me one look and in that one look
your eyes told me everything my heart wanted to hear
one look says it all

One look says it all
one look says it all
one look says it all
says it all.

"Knowledge Is Power"

Knowledge is power it can take us very far
it's the foundation on which civilization is constructed
there it presently stands as it lifts and propels us
as we boldly venture into the future

It is the pivot on which the world revolves
it can take us individually and collectively
in any direction
to any horizon or dimension to which we set our minds
we are now journeying beyond the sky

Knowledge is power in this the age of information
knowledge is an infinite gold mine
it is continuing to expand into the millennium
and beyond
let your thirst for knowledge never end

Knowledge, knowledge is power
so do not idle away your spare hours use them wisely
get an education and the power to move the world
you will put at your disposal

Now remember knowledge "knowledge is power"
yes "knowledge is power"
knowledge is power
knowledge is power.

You Are Too Sweet

You are too sweet the bees are not pleased
they will like to know the reason why
why should you be sweeter than they are
you have got their honeycomb in an uproar

Sweet too sweet you are too sweet
I love you and I will continue to love you
even if you become sweeter
but that will never happen
'cause you are as sweet as you will ever be sugar

You are too sweet those words
you will never hear coming from my lips
don't worry with those bees they are just peeved
because you are much sweeter than they are
by far my dear

Sweet too sweet still I love you as you are
have got a sweet tooth I love you sugar
too sweet too sweet not for me I love you sugar
am addicted I need you constantly and forever

Sweet you are too sweet you are too sweet
too sweet! ha ha too sweet come here
I want you sugar
I love you you are too sweet
forever be my sugar.

In an Intimate Embrace

We are locked in an intimate embrace
and our hearts refuse to unfold for we know
this love this romance of ours is going to last forever
so unfolding will simply be a complete waste of time

In an intimate embrace
we are locked in an intimate embrace
and this loving is driving us over the edge
driving us over the edge of our mind

We are locked in an intimate embrace
we are in an intimate embrace and our hearts refuse to
once again become single after all this time of being
locked together in an intimate embrace

We are in an intimate embrace
we are locked in an intimate embrace
and this love we are making
this love we are making is driving us wild
yes we are going crazy with this love we are making

In an intimate embrace we are locked
in an intimate embrace
there's no way our hearts
are going to let go of each other
this romance this love of ours is destined to last forever
in an intimate embrace we are enfolded
til the end of time

Till the end of time
our hearts are enfolded
in an intimate embrace
in an intimate embrace.

She's Got Fashion Sense

She's got fashion sense
she does not follow she's the leader
she's a setter of brand new trends
she's taking fashion in new directions
to new dimensions

Glamorous graceful exciting and elegant
she's always on the cutting edge
in the fashion business where the crowds now headed
she has long since been

She's got fashion sense
she does not follow fashion she sets trends
she's at the pinnacle in this business of fashion design
she's the standard of everyone's aspiration in fashion

Glamorous and graceful elegant and exciting
style flair and flamboyance she's everything in fashion
she's a model of magnificence she's got fashion sense
she's got fashion sense

She got fashion sense
fashion sense.

Come Home

Come home honey don't do this to us
don't break us up don't break our hearts
why keep us apart don't you know our love
our love has to last a lifetime

Going out on your own again will not solve the problem
why are we blowing this way out of proportion
let's get back together on common ground
let's find where we are going wrong and make it right

Come home honey think about our children
don't break us up please don't do this to us
you will be breaking our hearts and keeping us apart
life's too short for us to keep carrying on like this

On your own again going out on your own again
think about it you think it will solve the problem
come let's find a way to understand
where each of us is coming from
then we can make amends

Come home honey I need you as much
as you need me
I see you are shaking your head on this we both agree
so let's start over this time we will see eye to eye
and never let things go awry come home hon

Come home.

Feel the Heat

I can feel the heat of your passion
even when you are away from me so strong
is its intensity
I can feel the heat of your passion
'cause it enfolds me completely

When you are here
in my arms loving me it warms
when you go away
the heat of your passion always stays with me

I can feel the heat of your passion
even when you are away from me very intense
is its intensity
I can feel the intense heat of your passion
even when you are away from me

Here in my arms when you are here
in my arms loving me
your loving increases my temperature exponentially
when you go away the heat of your passion
always remains with me

I can feel it yes I can feel the heat
feel the heat of your passion constantly
I can feel the heat the heat of your passion
I can feel the heat the heat of your passion

The heat of your passion.

Don't Despair

Don't despair when you feel like
your world is coming apart and there's
nothing you can do to keep it together
just let it go and turn away

Tomorrow is another day
look inside yourself and find
a beautiful memory of a time
when things was going your way
on that memory let your mind stay

Don't despair because forever nothing remains
the same way
changes for the better can be found in each new day
trouble has to pass away
in tomorrow if you look into tomorrow
you will find a better way

Tomorrow is always another day
turn and walk away
whenever the day is not going your way
look into tomorrow
there happiness is waiting seize it bring it your way

Don't despair happiness is always there
look for it don't let it slip away unnoticed
look for it and it will look your way
bring it your way

Don't despair.

Magical Mysterious Magnificent

You are magical you are mysterious you are magnificent
intriguing you have got my heart beating like lightening
I can't stop thinking about you the only thing
I want to do is to always be with you

Have seen you around before
still I don't really know you
just keep observing you from afar
like to make your acquaintance
so that we can get to know each other much better

Magical you are magical you are mysterious
you are truly magnificent intriguing
you have got my heart
beating like lighten night and day it's the same thing
can't stop thinking about you

Seen you around before
am growing tired of just casually observing you from afar
I will really like to get to know you
so that we can get much closer
where we can we go from there

Where can we go from there
only our hearts in time will reveal the answer
you are magical mysterious and magnificent
not much longer don't leave me to keep wondering
about you

magical mysterious magnificent
you are all those things
and am always thinking about you
magical mysterious magnificent.

Living a Colorful Life

Am living a colorful life
have got splendor in my eyes body heart
soul and mind
yes life is a celebration and I am celebrating mine
am celebrating mine how about you

I know this celebration has a specified amount of time
still the end cannot be known beforehand
so I do not want to run out of time
am packing every moment
with miles of smiles enthusiasm and joy

Am living a colorful life
have got splendor all around it's in the silvery moon
which adorns the night sky along with
the sparkling stars and the
golden sun glittering on the horizon
every precious morn

This celebration I know this life of mine
has a specified amount of time
still the end will come when it will come
so I am packing every moment with miles of smiles
don't want the end to catch me wearing a frown

Am living a colorful life
have got no time for feeling down
life's a celebration and am celebrating mine
everyday am celebrating mine

Am living a colorful life.

A Good Thing

Wait on me and a good thing
I will soon be bringing to you
from now to eternity you will never have
any problems with me
you will see just you wait on me

Am a good thing and if you wait
I will be bringing myself to you
no you don't have to wait forever
soon I will soon be bringing myself to you

Wait on me and a good thing
I will soon be bringing to you from now to eternity
you won't have to worry I will always make you happy
it won't be a waste of time if you wait on me

Am a good thing and if you wait
for your patience you will be handsomely
rewarded with me
so wait I won't be late soon very soon
I will soon be bringing myself to you

"good things comes to those who wait" remember
so wait on me and you will have a good thing forever
am a good thing soon I will deliver myself
and all my love to you
to you I will soon be delivering a good thing

Wait on me am coming soon.

Romantically Inclined

Our hearts are romantically inclined
I know it won't be too long
before we find that they are entwined
entwined deep in a once in a lifetime love

Your heart and mine
they are showing all the signs of becoming involved
involved in a deep romantic
exciting and everlasting love

Our hearts are romantically inclined
in our eyes it is showing without a doubt
it's making us innocently smile with each other
from time to time
it has to happen we will fall in love

Your heart and mine no matter how we try to hide
they are showing all the signs
they are showing all the signs of beginning
to fall in love
yes our hearts they are romantically inclined

Our hearts are romantically inclined
romantically inclined.

Go Back to School

Go back to school
no it's not uncool to go back to school
dropping out only guarantees
that you will become a big flop
it reduces your options contracts your horizons
and leads you in the direction of
dead ending destinations

Go back to school
because it's very unusual for someone without
a good education to break out from the ruts
education propels you as you reach for the top

Go back to school
knowledge is a basic requisite of life
without it you won't know where to begin
and you would have already been left behind

Go back to school
education is a tool and in this life it is a must
it is very important that you are educated
so don't fool around with your education
go back to school

Go back to school learn all you can
pay attention look listen and learn
learn all you can go back to school
get an education.

You Are an Original

You are an original
yes you are unique a masterpiece
if you should search this vast universe
am sure another like you, you will never find

A one and only that's what you are for sure
so why this urge to follow the crowd
trying to be like they are
or whatever they dictate to you
be yourself and remember you are your hero

You are an original
a masterpiece yes you are unique
am positive yes I am very sure
if you should search the world over
it will be impossible to find any other like you

A one and only
only you can be you no one else is suitable
likewise you can never be anyone else
you simply have to be who you are yes you

Why be an imitation
when you are already the real thing
yes you are an original
stand up and be counted be proud to be who you are

Be you and you are an original.

A Cell of Your Love

Am imprisoned in a cell of your love
and it is getting smaller with each passing moment
that we are together
soon these walls will disappear and only
your arms will be holding me close to your heart

Love is holding me prisoner
and I am a model inmate I have accepted my fate
from the cell of your love forever
I will never make any attempt to escape

Am imprisoned in a cell of your love
and every moment that we are together
like handcuffs your love is getting tighter and tighter
keeping me secure in your heart

Love is holding me prisoner
your love is holding me tighter and am not a fighter
have completely surrendered to my fate
lock up your heart throw the key away
never let me escape

Am imprisoned in a cell of your love and forever
here in your heart I will stay
am imprisoned in a cell
a cell of your love.

My Perpetual Obsession

You are my perpetual obsession
although we have been together forever
I will never tire of and begin treating you
with indifference
always I will always treat you with love

From the day we met into perpetuity don't expect
my love to grow any stronger than it was on that day
for all that you want it to be it is already
don't expect it to become any stronger

You are yes you are my perpetual obsession
no matter how many forevers we are together
forever I will forever be perpetually obsessed with you
really and truly am in for eternity

My perpetual obsession no other attraction
will ever become my obsession
no other attraction can distract and arouse
this burning passion
which you perpetually keep arousing in me

My perpetual obsession
you are my perpetual obsession
perpetual obsession.

Hear Your Voice

I can only hear your voice on the telephone line
but that only frustrates my mind
and makes me more lonely for you
why do I only have to listen and not be able to
see your face and put my arms around you

I hate telephones and its lines
which keeps me in touch
while still keeping us at an infinite distance
you are on my mind and on the telephone line
when I need you in my arms

I can only hear your voice on the telephone line
my mind expands to envelop you
then my heart instantly becomes extremely lonely
and I suffer in silence

I hate this telephone and all of its lines
for they keep playing tricks on me
they keep me connected while still
separating you from me and am dying inside

I can only hear your voice
but am longing to see and
put my arms around you something which I cannot do
through this telephone line

bye.

Waiting for You in My Mind

Am waiting for you in my mind because
in my mind I keep meeting you night after night
still I cannot hold you in my arms and that's
where I really want you

Time is running wild and am still stuck here in time
meanwhile am running out of time
when will we meet so that
I can take you in my arms and love you

Am waiting for you in my mind
for in my mind in the night
is where I keep meeting you
am always meeting you in my mind in the night
and in real life in the daylight I cannot hold you

Time is running wild and am frozen in time
stuck here in no man's land and
I need you here with me
am running out of time while time is running wild
where are you
will I ever hold you in my arms before
time runs out on me

Am waiting for you in my mind
come to me hurry please come to me
come to me before time runs out on me
am waiting for you in my mind and
I don't have much time.

Your Heart Is My Accomplice

Your heart is my accomplice in this love
we cannot do it alone but together
we can build a love that's much stronger
than any the world has ever known

Together we can do this come let's give it a try
let's build a love which will be the envy
of lovers the world over
because forever and beyond the end of time
it will belong to you and I

Your heart is my accomplice in this love
alone it's impossible for either one of us to accomplish
together we can build it
build a love that's much stronger
than any the world has ever known

Together we can do it yes together we can build it
let's give it a try let's build a love
which can outlast time
your heart is my accomplice
together we can accomplish it let's build it together

Your heart is my accomplice.

Part Invitation Part Intimidation

That's a strange look
which you have got in your eyes
part invitation part intimidation and I am
sitting here wondering whether am to be invited
or intimidated

Am a gambling man and am
inviting myself into your arms
once am there you can welcome or you
can begin to intimidate me am up to the challenge

It's a strange look you have got
you have got a strange look in your eyes
part intimidation part invitation
am sitting here spellbound
wondering if am to be invited or intimidated by you

Am taking the chance am reading that look
in your eyes as an invitation
I am inviting myself into your arms
if am right welcome me into your heart
if am wrong then you are free to intimidate me
till kingdom come

That look in your eyes
that look in your eyes is a big challenge.

Don't Keep Your Passion Bottled Up Inside

Don't keep your passion bottled up inside
don't keep it all bottled up inside no don't
let it out girl don't hold it until it explodes
let it out let your passion freely slide

Why control or try to control it
isn't it what's it all about
passion by its very name implies a fire running wild
so let it destroy your inhibitions let it do
as its name implies

Don't keep it don't keep your passion bottled up
inside
don't keep it all bottled up inside no don't
let it out girl don't hold it too long or it will explode
let it out girl let it freely slide don't keep it inside

Why control it like a river it must be run free
give expression to your passion or it will find a way
and when it's all said and done you will be left
wondering what happened
passion must be given expression

I can see it in your eyes feel it in your heartbeat
hear it in your voice still you keep
repressing and refusing to give expression
to your passion
defy convention stop being so upright give expression

Give expression to your passion
stop trying to deny its existence
give expression to your passion
give expression to your passion.

Have Got a Guilty Conscience

Have got a guilty conscience
which is tearing at my mind
am not suppose to be in love with you
but I am and have been for quite a very long time

You belong to a very good friend of mine
so any hope of us getting together
is totally out of the question
still I can't get you out of my mind

Have got a guilty conscience
which is tearing at my mind you are not
making it easy on me
'cause every time we meet you keep giving me
a big smile with this come on look in your eyes

You belong to a very good friend of mine
still you are trying to drive me wild
any hope of us getting together
get them out of your mind
still you are where you should not be

Yes you are on my mind
but that's out of the question
have got a guilty conscience
how will I look my friend in the eye
sorry have got a guilty conscience

Have got a guilty conscience.

This Thing of Ours

This thing of ours how long
do you think we can keep it a hidden secret
how long can we keep meeting secretly
before everyone gets to know about it

Am getting tired of hiding and meeting
in dark corners in strange places
we are in love and in the light of day
together we can never show our faces

This thing of ours why do we keep hiding it
sooner or later someone is sure to notice
this thing of ours how long again
do you think we can keep it a hidden secret

This thing of ours yes this affair
this love affair of ours what are you afraid of
how long are you planning to keep it a secret
am tired of hiding

Tell me don't you think it's time
time we bring it out in the open
we are big people this thing this love affair of ours
sooner or later everyone is going to know about it

Everyone will know that we are together
so why are we still playing hide and seek.

Slippery When Wet

The sign said slippery when wet proceed with caution
I don't know what caused her distraction
but she did not notice until she slipped
and fell into my arms

We did not know it then
but her fall was the beginning of our romance
'cause since that day
she has not left the safety of these rescuing arms

The sign read slippery when wet proceed with caution
maybe she was pressed for time and
did not notice the sign
until she realized she had already fallen
into these arms of mine

She did not read the sign
could it be that she had it all planned all the time
for when she fell and I held her not for a moment
did I ever notice a look of surprise in her eyes

Slippery when wet proceed with extreme caution
not responsible if you should fall in love
not responsible if your heart should get broken
that's what the sign should now read
because that's exactly what happened

Proceed with extreme caution
slippery when wet.

Take Action

Take action because nothing ever happens
without action
without action even the best laid plans
will forever lay in wait always remaining
a figment of its creators imagination

Nothing ever happens without action
take action words of themselves can provide motivation
but they cannot put plans into construction
only you can bring plans into realization

Take action because nothing ever happens without action
begin initiate start activate they are just words
unless you begin to take action
to demonstrate their meaning
they of themselves cannot do anything

Nothing ever happens if you don't make it happen
take action without action
even a master plan is a mirage
which with the passing of time moves further and
further from realization

Take action if you have got a plan
don't waste any more time
begin to take action right now
beat the iron while your plan is hot
take action right now
what are you waiting for take action now

Take action take action take action.

Enthusiasm

Enthusiasm is the motor in motivation
it encourages and empowers you
as you set your sights beyond the stars
aims high and strives for excellence

Enthusiasm builds self confidence
opens your eyes to new possibilities
expands your horizon and gives you
an exciting and exhilarated feeling

Enthusiasm is the fuel
which fires ambition and
perpetually propels you in a
forward onward and upward direction

Necessity may be the mother of invention
but without the father called enthusiasm
all you will be left with is
stillborn ideas in your imagination

Enthusiasm is most essential
it is the principal element
in your quest for success
so with enthusiasm begin to take action now.

Smile It's Catching

Smile it's catching smile spread it all around
smile let it fall and someone will catch and pass it on
and another will pass it on and so on
smile it gives you a wonderful feeling

When you smile and it pass on to another
then another catches it and passes it on
in no time at all you can have the whole world
smiling and expressing joy

Smile it's catching see look you are smiling
look they are smiling too see it's working
everyone's smiling just because you started smiling
smile continue smiling yes smile it's catching

When you smile and pass it on
then another catches it and passes it on
in no time at all you can have the whole world
feeling very good smiling and expressing joy

So smile and pass it on don't keep it hidden
there's lots more where it came from
smile spread it all around let it fall someone will
catch and pass it on to another and they will pass it on

Smile and in no time at all
as your smile is passed on pretty soon your smile
will reach out and touch the world
and everyone will join in
expressing their joy

Yes everyone will smile
smile reach out and touch the world
smile yes smile it's catching
I see you are smiling and that's a beautiful thing.

Clear the Air

Let's clear the air
we cannot keep going on this way
am talking to you and you are
just ignoring me and each and every word I say

What's happening here
how did we ever get this way
it's not suppose to be like this
between you and me

Let's clear the air
once and for all say what you have to say
let me hear what's the problem
this has gone on for much too long

What is really happening here
is it something I have done or did not do
maybe something I said and should not have said
am all ears what's the reason for this silent treatment

Let's clear the air
let's bring everything out in the open
your silent treatment has the air stuffy in here
say what you must please clear the air

Let's once and for all
let's clear the air.

We Are Number One

We are number one in the universe
the runner up is light-years behind us
if you are seeking excellence see us first
no one else can even come close to us

The cream of the crop that's what we are
we are the top from afar you can clearly see us
we stand head and shoulders above all the rest
we are yes indeed we are we are the very best

We are number one in the universe the also ran
don't even come close to us they are trying their best
yet in their hearts they are aware that we are the best
they will have to be contented and settle
for second place

The cream of the crop the commander-in-chief
the numero uno the head honcho the C.E.O.
the summit the very pinnacle the model of excellence
that's what we are yes sir we are number one
 we are number one

We are number one, we are number one,
we are number one.

The Road to Success

The road to success is paved with goal
having a goal puts you on a roll
it is a stepping stone which motivates and
moves you along
helps you to persevere and keep traveling on

The road to success is paved with goal
but to get there you got to be prepared
to leave the safety of your comfort zone
hey why are you still hanging around

The road to success is paved with goal
set one up, get to it, make it a milestone
pass or achieve it
then begin again set another one

The road to success is paved with goal
it is the beacon which will guide direct and give you
the desire and determination
to triumphantly reach your destination

Yes! the road to success
is paved with goal
the road to success
is paved with goal.

Reach for Your Future

Reach for your future aim higher
hitch your thoughts to a star
persevere and it will take you from where you are
straight to wheresoever you desire

Reach for your future
break out from the routine and the familiar
motivate yourself to escape your limitations
go beyond your comfort zone discover new horizons

Reach for your future
tomorrow and the day after don't have to be
similar to today and the day which went before
change tomorrow dream a big dream today

Reach for your future
there's no reason for you to be caught in a rut
when it is possible for you to escape
to a new dimension
but the decision is up to you are you ready
do you want to

Reach for your future.

Sexy Seductive Sensual

She's sexy she's seductive she's sensual
just by looking at you she can
make your imagination run wild and never stop
until she's in your arms

Your heart she can charm and take your soul too
be careful if you see her looking at you
look away or she will take you
wherever she wants to

She's sexy she's seductive she's sensual
just by looking at her in the blink of an eye
she can have you eating out your heart
begging her to do whatever she wants

Her eyes are magnets look into them and they will
securely hold you to her
when she smiles and turns on her charm
never again will you ever be your own man
you have been warned

She's sexy she's seductive she's sensual
sexy sensual seductive.

This Is Your Moment

This is your moment the spotlight's on you
you are at centre stage looking adorable
revel in your glory girl everything you dreamed of
is finally coming true

In the beginning your dream
seemed far out of reach still that never deterred you
congratulations you kept reaching for your dream
now your dream is reaching out to you

This is your moment the spotlight's now on you
take a bow yes acknowledge your adoring crowd
you deserve all the accolades
they are showering on you

Wipe that tear from your eyes
tonight the only tears you should be shedding
are tears of joy smile smile glow in the spotlight
revel in the glory of your moment you have earned it

Yes this is your moment
this is your moment
this is your moment.

Fresh Look

You have got this fresh look about you
so innocent and so new
like a morning rising on the horizon
you look so full of promise so golden

Never let it desert you
although time may not obey you
keep that fresh look
even when it becomes an outlook

You have got this fresh look about you
so innocent and so new
like a morning rising over the horizon
you look so full of promise so unrestricted

Never let it desert you
although time will not obey you
keep that fresh look even when it becomes an outlook
you have got this fresh look about you

You have got this fresh look.

Achievers

Achievers are ordinary people
who always do a little extra then when others
have thrown in the towel and fallen by the wayside
enthusiastically they willingly go the extra mile

Achievers are ordinary people
who are not contented with the status quo
mediocrity is not what they will settle for
when they know they can do so much better

Achievers are ordinary people
who do not settle for less for what's good enough
for it's passible for them the best
excellence is what they are always striving for

Achievers are ordinary people
who do more expect more and eventually receive more
they always exceed what's required of themselves
that's why achievers are extraordinary people
achievers are extraordinary people.

A Dream Denied

A dream denied never dies
if the dreamer has the temerity
to keep the fire of desire burning
in their hearts and in their eyes

A dream denied can and will be realized
but the dreamer of the dream
must turn blind eyes to obstacles and setbacks
and keep their eyes on the prize

A dream denied is still a dream
the dreamer has to keep alive
its time may have not yet arrived
by taking action it will begin to materialize

A dream denied never dies
if the dreamer perseveres
sooner rather than later
their dream is sure to be realized

A dream denied can never die
unless the dreamer
by neglecting to keep on dreaming
forfeits its life

A dream never dies.

If You Want It

If you want it if you really want my love
you have got to do better than that
if you really want it you just cannot skim the surface
you have got to dig way down deep in my heart

It's priceless it is precious
that's why I cannot leave it hanging around
if you really want it you will find it there
if you want it you will surely find it

If you want it if you really want it
if you truly want my love you have got to do
much better than this
you just can't skim the surface and expect to find it
you got to dig way deep down in my heart

It's priceless it's precious
I just cannot leave it hanging around
where anyone can swipe it if you really want it
dig deep it's worth it when you find it treasure it

If you want it you will find it
if you really want my love you will have patience
if you want it you won't turn and run
saying it's too hard to find

You really want it then you have got to
dig way down deep in my heart
if you really want my love
you have got to dig way down deep in my heart.

With You in Mind

Am living my life with you in mind
and in the meantime
am devising ways in which
I can make you mine

Have been trying for a very long time
to get close to you now I find
that I have only been wasting my time
for this time was not yet the right time
for you and me

Am still living my life with you in mind
and the ways which am devising to make you mine
am positive yes am absolutely certain
they are going to work this time

Have been trying for a very long time
now I will make this time the right time
this time has got to be
be the right time for you and me

Am living my life with you in mind
and the ways which am devising
to make you mine this time
this time they are going to work

Am going to make you mine this time
tired of living with you in mind
living my life with you in mind
with you in mind.

Where Friends Meet

I met her where friends meet
now we are so much more than friends
we are even more than just good friends
we are having meetings heart-to-heart

A chance encounter a hesitant glance
brought us together now here I am
all taken in yes am totally smitten
I want to be with her forever

I met her where friends meet and we
could not take our eyes off of each other
she greeted me with a smile as wide as the horizon
and I was a goner

A chance encounter brought us together
now we cannot stand
to be away from each other
not even for a moment

Where friends meet that's where we met
now forever we want to be together
'cause now we are so much more than friends
much more than friends.

High and Dry

You left me high and dry
now what am I to do without
the love of my life who promised to love and be
with me till the end of time

Like a river overflowing its banks
water is now flooding my eyes
my heart's barren and dry as a desert
'cause you are no longer living inside

You left me high and dry
now am without the love of my life
from the daylight I want to run and hide
I don't want to show my face even in the night

High and dry you used to take me
to such great heights
now you left me high and dry and I
am falling further and further down into despair
as water continues flowing in my eyes

High and dry you left me high and dry
now am feeling down all the time
you left me high and dry
now tears are in my eyes all the time.

It's Now Overdue

It's now overdue
your love is now overdue
right now this instant if it's not delivered to me
I cannot tell what the consequences would be

Bring it immediately
I don't want to suffer the consequences of not
having it near me
why are you withholding it
I need it bring it to me in a hurry

It's now overdue
your love is now overdue
right now this moment if it's not delivered to me
my heart tells me the consequence will be severe

Bring it to me immediately
am on fire have got high fever
don't let me suffer any longer stop holding it
baby instantly immediately bring your love to me

Now overdue
your love is now overdue.

Coming Soon

It's coming soon just a little longer
yes stay right where you are
don't move wait just a little longer
coming soon it's coming soon

I know it seems like
you have been waiting on it forever
remember what they say about patience being virtue
it's true so relax

It's coming soon I can reassure you
have got inside information
I know it won't be too long again
cause it's coming soon

It seems like you have been
waiting on it forever hold on don't move
you cannot give up now just a while longer
any moment now love is going to be here
don't despair hold on

Love is coming soon it's coming soon
love is coming soon love is soon coming your way
coming soon love is coming to you very soon
coming soon.

All of a Sudden

All of a sudden
I can't stop thinking of you
I can't stop thinking of you all of a sudden
what have you got happening to me all of a sudden

How long have I known you casually
and what is happening to me
never ever even hinted of happening to me now
all of a sudden
suddenly it's happening to me all of a sudden

All of a sudden
I can't stop thinking of you
I just can't stop thinking of you all of a sudden
what have you done to make me keep thinking of you

Like vines on a tree you have grown on me
now all of a sudden you are on my mind constantly
all of a sudden suddenly all of a sudden
you are on my mind constantly

All of a sudden you are on my mind constantly
girl what have you done to me
all of a sudden
all of a sudden am in love with you.

A Passion for Learning

In this the school of life
you have got to develop a passion for learning
for in this supersonic age
everything changes in haste

And your knowledge of yesterday
will tomorrow become antiquated, outdated,
not up to speed
and therefore obsolete and unable to
assist you in your drive to succeed

With a passion for learning
your thirst and appetite for ongoing knowledge
will constantly be sated as learning becomes fun
and therefore done easily

It is said daily "knowledge is power"
and daily life is becoming
more and more dependent on banks of data so as not
to be outdone by those banks of mainframe
and micro computers

You need to develop a passion for learning
constantly keep refreshing the data
in your own computer
keep refreshing your brain with new
and relevant knowledge
which is appropriate for this day and age

Develop a passion for learning
a passion for learning.

More to You Than Meets the Eye

There's more to you than meets the eye
if anyone had told me
you were this intriguing this amazing
surely I would have told them they are telling lies

You are full of nice little surprises
some of the things you do really astonishe me
have never seen this side of you before
and it makes me love you more

There's more to you that meets the eye
and to tell the truth if we weren't formally introduced
I would have never given you a second look or thought
then that would have been my loss

You are full of surprises
you sure had me fooled looking so quiet
and unassuming
but beneath your demure disguise
you are one steaming sensual woman

Am glad to have made your acquaintance
but that's all past tense we are beyond that
we are something much more that friends
lovers yes we are lovers

There sure is there is much more to you
there's more to you than meets the eye
more to you than meets the eye
more there's more to you than meets the eye.